SELF CARE
A New Normal

A 30 DAY CHALLENGE
PERSONAL JOURNAL

WWW.HEALTHYLIFESTYLECOACHING.ORG
Beach Life in Scarborough, Maine

Edited by: Jean Shorey and Alicia Girard

Published by: GWN Publishing

www.GWNPublishing.com

Cover Design: Kristina Conatser Captured by KC Design

ISBN: 979-8-9859746-8-3

Dedication

My father was neither an anchor

to hold me back,

nor a sail to take me there

but always a guiding light

whose love showed me the way.

Contents

"Don't be the *sail* in the breeze; *be the breeze*"

Introduction to an Ocean Theme

How often do you dream about living in a new normal lifestyle right now? Maybe It could be your inner desire to change a little part of you to be healthier and happier. Thinking back before the pandemic our reality was living a balanced life and being in control of our own world of surviving. Our self-care was not comprised or depleted in the old normal world we lived in. So now this leaves us in the here and now to refocus on renewal, regeneration and healing.

The changes you make need a plan to guide you to stay the course and develop long term benefits. Offering an Invitation to join me in the 30-day challenge to start your own self-care journey now. My motto; **"Don't be the sail in the breeze; be the breeze"** has guided me to use the ocean treasures and keep an imaginary focus and vision on self-care needs.

THE OCEAN TREASURES ARE:

THE SAILBOAT is the vessel you can use to sail in your journey to becoming a new you! Open your sails wide to feel the breeze!

LIGHT HOUSES can symbolize challenges, adversity or guidance. The symbol can also mean keeping alert under dire circumstances.

STARFISH symbolizes renewal and regeneration. Trust your instincts and follow your star. Be resourceful, empathic, patient and insightful.

ANCHOR is a device that can give you a strong hold for the self-care goals you seek.

SEA SHELLS have gentle and healing energy which works with the healer to cleanse, balance, and harmonize. Shells can heal and regenerate ourselves.

SEAGRASSES are known as the "lungs of the sea. Relating or comparing seagrass to our human needs is one of detoxification.

SAND DOLLAR, the legend of this shell is Christian based through the five defining slits. When the shell is broken five small but perfect replicas of a dove will be found. The doves representing peace and serenity.

Defining Self-Care

Self-care is taking care of one's self in order to live a productive and meaningful life. Self-care is not self-indulgence or selfish. The attainment of self-care often defies many variables. Knowing how to achieve a higher quality of life; even when faced with such variables as a serious illness, a medical condition or being the sole caregiver of a loved one. One significant variable is the sudden introduction of a world-wide pandemic such as COVID-19. The crucial question becomes, "How do I practice a daily self-care routine when faced with so many variables in the world today? Coping with the stress and uncertainty of this pandemic has brought on a tremendous amount of emotional distress. We all created a "new normal" lifestyle including new routines at home, work, school, and in our social life.

Let's focus on a NEW SELF-CARE perspective in healing our bodies, minds and spirit. We can begin to make changes big or small. Living with our old habits of self-care in our current lifestyle is a major change. Many of us lived a fast-paced life; constantly trying to find time just to relax and breathe. Thinking back to what we thought a normal rhythm in our lives was may not have included quality time to enjoy family gatherings, raising children, social events or vacations. The world has come to a standstill. We have no choice but to remain in self-isolation or in our own "quarantine bubble". We have adjusted and realized that the normal pace of life is having the time for true self-care. The valuable gift of time has bridged the self-care journey with the new mindset of living your best life. Don't look behind you look forward. Appreciate the good things you accomplished since the beginning of the pandemic. Feel the peace and joy with all that you have accomplished with help from your family and friends. Your new self-care mindset now includes your "quarantine bubble "that defines the new you!

SELF-CARE is a personal goal of the 4 Components of Wellness. Everyone's approach will be different. We must focus and balance on what one does both at home and at work. Managing our total well-being is managing the total "Me". When this happens, we have a totally nourished body and a balanced life of self-care. Everyone can meet their personal and professional commitment to putting themselves first to achieve the best outcome.

One's reality check for practicing SELF-CARE must include taking an active role in protecting your well-being from stress, trauma, anxiety or sudden life changes. I would like to share some self-care components that were useful to many of my coaching clients.

PHYSICAL SELF-CARE is the state of health achieved through proper nutrition, exercise and rest

* Take and make time each day for relaxation

* Maintain and develop a good sleep routine

* Create daily well-balanced meal plans and snacks

* Hydrate well with water according to your body weight recommendations

* Take dedicated lunch breaks at work settings

* Take daily walks either at home or work

* Seek advice from a professional trainer to improve your cardio or flexibility workouts

* Engage in a non-work hobby or sport that you desirc

* Learn to turn off your emails and work phone

* Get adequate rest by having a scheduled regular bedtime routine

EMOTIONAL SELF-CARE is allowing yourself to safely experience your full range of emotions.

* Develop relationships that are supportive and nurturing

* Keep a daily gratitude or reflective journal

* Identify your stressors

* Play a sport that energizes and lowers your stress level

* Get rid of negativity in your life that holds you back

* Go to a movie or have a game night with friends or family to stay connected for your social well being

* Share with family or friends about how you're coping with your job or life's demands

* Try a massage, Reiki, Herbal baths, essential oils or other holistic natural remedies that reduce stress and anxiety

* Your emotional health is a gentle voice within you helping you become the best version of a healthier you!

* Choose your Happy ...and acknowledge that only you have control over yourself

SPIRITUAL SELF-CARE involves having a sense of perspective beyond your day-to-day life.

* Engage in reflective practices like meditation, mindfulness or spiritual music. Silent meditation for a few minutes is something that helps in restoring a sense of calm when we are stressed or have increased anxiety

* Practice yoga, reiki, stretching, massage, relaxation techniques and toning exercises

* Opening your heart is an essential aspect of true spirituality

* Identify to whom or what you are spiritually connected. Examples would be church family or bible study group
* Support partnership by helping each other achieve the day-to-day chores of homelife

INTELLECTUAL SELF-CARE is being open to new ideas, people, and beliefs that are different from your own

* Decreases our stress and anxiety levels
* Promotes peace and tranquility
* Reduces our susceptibility to burnout It has significant changes on our outlook on life
* Enhance and strengthen our resiliency
* When the mind, body and spirit are well nourished they then become balanced
* Energized, productive, restored health, disease prevention and healthy mindset
* Gather with friends and engage in conversations that are educational. Learn new ventures, skills or find a passion in your work life
* Take up a new hobby that inspires and reveals your creativity
* Daily readings on different cultures and places to vacation

Your Self-Care Journey

Is like

No

Other

Your personal goals

Are unique to You

Your Successes

can make a Difference

because only "You can be You"

"Your purpose is like a *lighthouse*. It guides you through difficult times so you can keep going forward."

—PATRICK HILL, PHD—

Know Your Why

Your why is the strongest reason for you to desire something. Finding your why can give you a sense of purpose to help you better weather life's ups and downs. Without purpose you can feel unmoored, as if something is missing in your life. Documented research has shown that having a purpose is critical to our overall health. Once you discover your why you become motivated to explore reasons that are beneficial in accomplishing your life goals.

Let's say you want to stop working and you go in business for yourself. Some possible why's; can be:

* Your why is financially security
* Your why has to be deep within when met with challenges
* Your why is a desire to own your own business and be independent
* Your why to satisfy a psychological need
* Your why is Quality family time
* Your why can physically energize
* Your why can enhance spirituality
* Your why can be to create that work life balance
* Your why can be simply helping others

If your why is big enough the how doesn't matter. Even if at the time you don't know how to achieve it or pursue it. By carrying out these two steps you will help sort out your personal definition of motivation. What motivates you? Can it be determination, success, dreams, ambition or fame?

STEP #1: Decide what you want. Be as clear as possible of what you want in a timely manner. Keeping faith is trusting in yourself. The most amazing things happen with faith within the journey because inner strength becomes stronger and dreams materialize!

STEP #2: Think about why you want it. Remember these have to be your strong reasons to desire the best in life! Stay strong because life's roughest storm proves the strength of your anchors! For those anchors remind you that one does best is tied to something that's solid and true.

Patrick Hill, PHD, an associate of psychological and brain science at Washington University in St. Louis states:

"Your purpose is like a lighthouse. It guides you through difficult times so you can keep going forward."

Changing a Daily Habit in 30 Days

There could be several reasons why we don't create positive change in our lives today. Could it be because we don't have a big enough desire to do it? Maybe it brings on the fear inside of us that we aren't capable of change. Fears such as; we set personal goals so big that they can't be reach; or we don't have that self-confidence or do we worry too much about what other people think of us?

Fears hides and lurks and blocks our way just as we are contemplating change in our lives. Firstly, we must address the fears that hold us back and affect us emotionally, physically, spirituality and intellectually. Secondly, once we do address the fear and conquer it then we are able to transition to make our desired change. Doing something different opens one -up to so many possibilities and creates that healthy life-style balance.

Change is powerful but it does take some effort on our part. Change can come into one's life as a result of a crisis, maybe by chance or even by choice. In either situation, many of us are faced with having to make a choice to make that change or continue an unhealthy pattern of progressively failing health.

I believe that it is better to be prepared for change because we have more control over how we react to change. When you are unprepared for change and are met with resistance then you have no control or even a choice to let go of that fear.

We cannot afford to avoid the unexpected crisis (events) in our lives, as it is these events that challenge us and force us to step out of our comfort zone. Taking that first step always seems the hardest. Always remember we are never alone in this world.

Changing a daily habit takes 30 days for one to see the benefits. So, ask yourself this question "What would changing a daily habit mean to me right now? Practicing good habits and making the right change keeps us strong and focused on our life goals. Providing self-care for ourselves daily helps us embrace those moments that bring us joy, healing and completeness.

Let us reflect on the FIVE STAGES that changing a daily habit can offer us, such as uplifting our spirit, providing daily self-care, motivating us to greater health, spiritual growth, gratitude, and recognition of oneself.

These are the FIVE STAGES that we go through to achieve healthy habits. It will take 30-days to develop new habits.

STAGE #1: **Pre-contemplation.** Maybe you think that a change would help but you're not certain if you are ready or even interested in change. This change you want to make may be too hard to make right now in your life.

Take some time to reflect on the *sand dollar* for it is said to be the coin of the ocean but actually a strong creature of the sea. Today you may make the essential lifestyle change you been waiting for!

STAGE #2: **Contemplation.** Now you are thinking or even recognizing a need to make a change.

Think about the *seashells* for they are the symbols of the sea that enhance one's mental clarity, create balance and prosperity. Let my self-care journey begin today!

STAGE #3: **Preparation.** You are ready to make a change within a month. You've made a realistic plan and done your homework to carry out your plan.

Your *sailboat* is ready to set sail and begin your new voyage! Stay strong and persevere for your sailboat will navigate your self-care journey.

STAGE #4: **Action.** Behavior change occurs. You have taken action and started your new routine. It's difficult at times and you are tempted to go back to your old habits.

Remember to stay the course and let the *lighthouse* be your beacon of light and guide you through any storms.

STAGE #5: **Maintenance.** You are used to your new routine after 3-6 months. It's now a habit. Relapse may occur and you need to use preventable measures to not go back to your old habits.

Hold onto to your *anchor* for it is your strength and stability that holds you in place no matter how rough things get!

Here is an example of mapping out your plan of changing habits below and how to get started. The first step is to think about what you need to change; an example is a health condition such as; diabetes, elevated cholesterol, emotional, pain management, mental health, or other medical conditions. (See above the 5 stages for more information that recaps questions to ask to begin your plan)

WHAT'S MY GOAL?

What change would help me reach my goal?

What stage am I in for this change?

* STAGE #1: I'm not ready to change right now
* STAGE #2: I'm thinking about doing it sometime
* STAGE #3: I might do it in the next month
* STAGE #4: I'm doing it now
* STAGE #5: I've been doing it for more than 6 months

Wellness Vision Tool Guide

The practical wellness vision tool becomes your personal statement that describes what you want to achieve as result of health issues or changing bad habits into good habits. It reflects the long-term values, behaviors, strategies, motivators, strengths and outcomes to live a healthy lifestyle. Once you complete your wellness vision tool and put it into practice you will see the benefits of accomplishing your set goals. Personally, this wellness tool has kept myself focused and dedicated to stay the course in the healing journey of my thyroid disorders. Often, what I found most rewarding as a health coach was helping individuals benefit from taking simple steps towards reaching their goals and embracing successes. Did I say this would be easy, absolutely not!

Here is the format that you can use in creating your **wellness vision** to complete a healing journey. Below are the examples to guide and inspire you in creating your own personal wellness vision.

WELLNESS VISION EXAMPLE: "In the next 6 months I have a healthy functioning thyroid gland and take a lower dose of thyroid medication. I will be twenty pounds lighter and regain my energy and resilience. I exercise regularly and eat 3 healthy meals every day." Your wellness vision is a compelling statement of who you are and what you want to achieve?

MY MOTIVATORS EXAMPLE: These are powerful reasons, values, desires, accomplishments that make your wellness vision very important to you. It will give you that motivation to make and sustain healthy behaviors. (Examples: I want to be healthy and fit to enjoy my family celebrations or I want to lose weight to fit into a size 12 dress.)

MY OBSTACLES: Your obstacles are the things that get in the way of living your best life or achieving your realistic goals. Some things maybe **obstacles:** busy work schedule, no family time, no transportation; limited finances. So, ask yourself this question, "What's getting in the way of living your wellness vision to "Be the best Version of Yourself."

STRATEGIES EXAMPLES: These are tactics that help you focus on your wellness vision, weight loss program, accomplish your goals or feel emotional balanced. Activities that help reach your goals are: Joining a gym 3 x week; drink 64oz water daily for weight loss; do my daily mediation; get together with family or friends for more socialization.

My Personal Wellness Vision Tool

MOTIVATORS. Reasons why embarking on this wellness journey is important to me now.

MY 3-MONTH GOAL(S). How I want my life to be better in 3 months.

STRENGTHS. Attributes that have helped me succeed in the past.

OBSTACLES. What gets in my way.	STRATEGIES TO OVERCOME OBSTACLES.

MY PLAN. Specific, measurable, attainable, realistic, and time-specific activities I will do.

Setting Your Smart Goals

Setting smart goals involves the development of an action plan designed in order to motivate, inspire, give direction and guide you toward a goal. Therefore, setting goals means that you have committed thought, emotion and behavior towards attaining the goal. Think of setting goals as the road map that guides you in the right direction to reach your goals.

* State goals so that they focus on specific things to do.
* Start small and take gradual steps to accomplish them.
* Start with something you can already do.
* Be realistic. Tailor goals to your own abilities and lifestyle
* Set measurable, attainable and time-bound goals
* Write down your goals to help you stay focused
* Setting goals are nothing without action, "Just do it"

"What you get by achieving your goals is not as important as what you become by achieving your goals."

ZIG ZIGLAR

SMART Goals Worksheet

S	Specific	What do I want to ultimately accomplish and how am I going to do it?
M	Measurable	How will I know that I have reached my goal?
A	Attainable	Can I break it down into manageable pieces?
R	Realistic	Is the goal too difficult to reach? Too easy?
T	Timely	What is my target date for reaching my goal?

Coaching Tips for Success in Life

1. **How you think is "Everything"!**
   Have a positive attitude. Think success, not failure.

2. **Set goals.**
   Write them down. Develop your plans to reach them.

3. **ACT.**
   Goals are nothing without action. Just do it!

4. **Learn.**
   Knowledge is power! Acquire skills and perfect them.

5. **Persist.**
   Success is a marathon, not a sprint. Don't give up!

6. **Analyze.**
   Consider opinions of others. Learn from your failures.

7. **Focus.**
   Don't let people or things distract you. Stay focused.

8. **Don't be afraid to innovate or be different.**
   Because only You can be You!

9. **Communicate effectively.**
   Speak and write clearly.

10. **Be honest and dependable; take responsibility...**
    or else Numbers from 1-9 will not matter.

Components of Wellness

The components of wellness encompass the physical, spiritual, intellectual and emotional needs to guide you through your 30 challenges. Making a commitment in practicing positive and healthy daily habits will help you to achieve a holistic approach to wellness.

"STRIVE FOR PROGRESS, NOT PERFECTION"

DAY 1

DATE: _____

Self-care is knowing how to achieve a higher quality of life even when you are faced with adversities. Begin today to create your true self-care wellness vision for a healthier you!

Your self-care wellness vision:
_____
_____
_____

Motivators:
_____
_____
_____

Obstacles:
_____
_____

Strategies:
_____
_____

Today's Goals:
_____
_____

Today's Accomplishments:
_____
_____

Learning new things or being in a place that are not familiar with you can sometimes be somewhat intimidating. Ask yourself this question "What would changing a habit mean to me right now in my life?

What one habit can you begin to change?

_____

_____

_____

Today's thoughts/reflections:

_____

_____

_____

Today's goals completed:

_____

_____

_____

Today's accomplishments/gratitude:

_____

_____

_____

DAY 3

DATE: _____

Know Your Why: because it is the strongest reason for you to want or desire something different. Begin your self-care journey today with these steps: #1 Decide what you want. Never mind how you are going to get there just decide what you want. #2 Think about Why you want it! These need to be your strongest reasons!

Know your why and write down your strongest reasons!

Today's thoughts/reflections:
_____
_____
_____
_____
_____

Today's goals completed:
_____
_____
_____
_____
_____

Today's accomplishments/gratitude:
_____
_____
_____
_____
_____

DATE: _____

Motivation is an important life skill. It would be difficult to achieve anything without it. Motivation is what moves you to action. Each individual is unique and has a purpose. One has to be motivated to work towards setting goals, making life plans and becoming successful.

What motivates you today?

_____

_____

_____

Today's thoughts/reflections:

_____

_____

_____

Today's goals completed:

_____

_____

_____

Today's accomplishments/gratitude:

_____

_____

_____

Setting goals gives you long-term vision and short-term motivation. Most important it focuses your acquisition of knowledge, guidance, planning and direction to reach your goals you want to set.

What direction did your goals take you today?

_____
_____
_____
_____

Today's thoughts/reflections:

_____
_____
_____
_____

Today's goals completed:

_____
_____
_____
_____

Today's accomplishments/gratitude:

_____
_____
_____
_____

DAY 6

Shape-up that Body! Movement of our bodies can be beneficial for the mental, spiritual and physical well-being. Don't hesitate to reach out for professional advice to design the right exercise program for you. Most important is that your personal workout helps you stay with it for the long-run and it's a critical part of your daily self-care routine!

Did your work-out energize you today?

_____

_____

_____

Today's thoughts/reflections:

_____

_____

_____

Today's goals completed:

_____

_____

_____

Today's accomplishments/gratitude:

_____

_____

The plate method is being mindful of a daily intake of nutritional meals of fruits, vegetables, grains, dairy and protein. The plate method is the key to maintain your health, feel good and have energy!

What healthy nutritional foods were on your plate today?

_____
_____
_____

Today's thoughts/reflections:

_____
_____
_____

Today's goals completed:

_____
_____
_____

Today's accomplishments/gratitude:

_____
_____
_____

DAY 8

DATE: _____

"*Stay Strong* because life's roughest storms prove the strength of your anchors. Capture your inner strength and persevere."

Name 5 strongest strengths you used today?
_____
_____
_____
_____

Today's thoughts/reflections:
_____
_____
_____
_____

Today's goals completed:
_____
_____
_____

Today's accomplishments/gratitude:
_____
_____
_____

DATE: _____

"Be Persistent as you rise above and beyond the challenge of this day, for this will be your most rewarding achievement!"

What was your persistent course of action today?

_____
_____
_____
_____

Today's thoughts/reflections:

_____
_____
_____
_____

Today's goals completed:

_____
_____
_____
_____

Today's accomplishments/gratitude:

_____
_____
_____
_____

DATE: _____

JUST DO IT! No one but you can make lifestyle changes. Don't wait another day because time will never be just the right moment!

What was one thing did you do today that was a JUST DO IT moment?
_____
_____
_____

Today's thoughts/reflections:
_____
_____
_____
_____

Today's goals completed:
_____
_____
_____
_____

Today's accomplishments/gratitude:
_____
_____
_____

Think Success because you will not only inspire yourself to become successful but inspire others as well!

What was a huge success for you today?
_____
_____
_____
_____

Today's thoughts/reflections:
_____
_____
_____
_____

Today's goals completed:
_____
_____
_____
_____

Today's accomplishments/gratitude:
_____
_____
_____
_____

DATE: _____

DAY 12

"Keeping a Positive Attitude can equip you with the tools you need to navigate your health journey in the most difficult storms."

What was a positive attitude skill you developed today?

_____
_____
_____
_____

Today's thoughts/reflections:

_____
_____
_____
_____

Today's goals completed:

_____
_____
_____
_____

Today's accomplishments/gratitude:

_____
_____
_____

DATE: _____

DAY 13

My coaching motto: *"Don't be the sail in the breeze. Be the Breeze".*

Is your self-care journey a breeze yet?

_____
_____
_____
_____

Today's thoughts/reflections

_____
_____
_____
_____

Today's goals completed:

_____
_____
_____
_____

Today's accomplishments/gratitude:

_____
_____
_____
_____

"Love Yourself First" ...this is your journey of self-care and self-acceptance.

What are some ways that you loved yourself in this challenge so far?

_____
_____
_____

Today's thoughts/reflections:

_____
_____
_____

Today's goals completed:

_____
_____
_____

Today's accomplishments/gratitude:

_____
_____
_____

DATE: _____

DAY 15

Keeping Faith is trusting in yourself. The most amazing things happen with faith within your journey because your inner strength becomes stronger.

Did your inner strength get you through the storm today?

_____
_____
_____
_____

Today's thoughts/reflections: _____

_____
_____
_____

Today's goals completed: _____

_____
_____
_____

Today's accomplishments/gratitude: _____

_____
_____
_____

DATE: _____

DAY 16

Keep your Sails Up! You are sailing in the right direction.

Today's thoughts/reflections:
_____
_____
_____
_____

Today's goals completed:
_____
_____
_____

Today's accomplishments/gratitude:
_____
_____
_____

DATE: _____

DAY 17

"Just Breathe" Try the 4-7-8 breathing technique of closing your mouth and inhale through your nose to the count of 4. Then hold your breath for a count of 7. Exhale completely through your mouth, making a whoosh sound to a count of 8.

How did that breathing technique work in releasing your stress and tension?

_____
_____
_____
_____

Today's thoughts/reflections:

_____
_____
_____
_____

Today's goals completed:

_____
_____
_____
_____

Today's accomplishments/gratitude:

_____
_____
_____
_____

DAY 18

"Let Your Light Shine" and keep it shining regardless of the roadblocks you encounter in the challenge today. Your individual shining essence has purpose, meaning, and a gift.

Did you let your inner light shine from barely bright to shining brightly today?

_____
_____
_____
_____

Today's thoughts/reflections:

_____
_____
_____
_____

Today's goals completed:

_____
_____
_____
_____

Today's accomplishments/gratitude:

_____
_____
_____
_____

DAY 19

"Believe in Yourself because this is the secret to reaching your goals successfully!"

Was there a successful goal that you embraced today?
_____
_____
_____
_____

Today's thoughts/reflections:
_____
_____
_____
_____

Today's goals completed:
_____
_____
_____
_____

Today's accomplishments/gratitude:
_____
_____
_____
_____

Practicing gratitude is one of the many positive emotions. It's about focusing on what's good in our lives and being appreciative of the things we have and not the things we don't have. Gratitude can change anyone's life because it is the most powerful source of inspiration that anyone can practice.

What is one reason gratitude can change your life?

_____
_____
_____
_____

Today's thoughts/reflections:

_____
_____
_____
_____

Today's goals completed:

_____
_____
_____
_____

Today's accomplishments/gratitude:

_____
_____

DAY **21**

DATE: _____

Embrace Your Success! Changing your lifestyle or unhealthy habits helps you move forward to be successful. It is the reward of success!

What one success did you embrace today?
_____
_____
_____
_____

Today's thoughts/reflections:
_____
_____
_____
_____

Today's goals completed:
_____
_____
_____
_____

Today's accomplishments/gratitude:
_____
_____
_____
_____

You're Not Alone! You may have trials and tribulations throughout your journey, but you are never without opportunities, guidance and support to become successful in your self-care challenge.

Who is that person you either met or had a conversation with today?

_____

_____

_____

Today's thoughts/reflections:

_____

_____

_____

_____

Today's goals completed:

_____

_____

_____

Today's accomplishments/gratitude:

_____

_____

_____

DAY 23

Weather the Storms! Sometimes you just have to ride the waves and meet the storms to experience something new and better. For it has been said when you come out of the storm you won't be the same person who went through it.

Have you experienced any storms in your life and asked yourself: how did I ever managed to survive it?

_____
_____
_____
_____

Today's thoughts/reflections:

_____
_____
_____
_____

Today's goals completed:

_____
_____
_____
_____

Today's accomplishments/gratitude:

_____
_____
_____

DATE: _____

DAY **24**

"No Regrets" Your only regrets are the changes you should have made!

What is your one biggest regret and how could you have changed it?

_____
_____
_____

Today's thoughts/reflections:

_____
_____
_____
_____

Today's goals completed:

_____
_____
_____

Today's accomplishments/gratitude:

_____
_____
_____

DATE: _____

My stress-free lifestyle begins with maintaining healthy habits. Less work; more play; have a hobby; have a positive attitude; be kind to yourself and others.

What are some ways you have been living a stress-free life?

_____
_____
_____
_____

Today's thoughts/reflections:

_____
_____
_____
_____

Today's goals completed:

_____
_____
_____
_____

Today's accomplishments/gratitude:

_____
_____
_____

DAY 26

Your *inner wisdom* is a gift of yourself that tells you what the world is saying. Listen to the wisdom of your body and trust your gut instinct. Have faith in your inner wisdom. It is working behind the scenes on your behalf to accomplish those personal goals.

What ways have you accessed your inner wisdom in doing this 30-day challenge?

_____

_____

_____

_____

Today's thoughts/reflections:

_____

_____

_____

Today's goals completed:

_____

_____

_____

Today's accomplishments/gratitude:

_____

_____

_____

DAY 27

DATE: _____

Establishing *good healthy habits* is beginning and ending each day with gratitude. Keep an ongoing food journal of your well balance meals; exercise workouts; daily hydration of water and a bedtime routine. Maintaining good healthy habits can be positive and the most successful change!

What are the 5 healthy habits you have acquired since starting your 30-day challenge?

_____

_____

_____

_____

Today's thoughts/reflections:

_____

_____

_____

_____

Today's goals completed:

_____

_____

_____

_____

Today's accomplishments/gratitude:

_____

_____

DATE: _____

DAY **28**

"Go with the waves..." for life will not always go as you have planned, for tides go in different directions. You cannot stop the waves but you can learn to move with them. They may not take you in the direction you planned but they will take you exactly where you are meant to be!

Where did your waves take you today?
_____
_____
_____
_____

Today's thoughts/reflections:
_____
_____
_____
_____

Today's goals completed:
_____
_____
_____
_____

Today's accomplishments/gratitude:
_____
_____
_____

Look within to see your *glowing image* and see the new you! Embrace this moment for all your hard work. What is one inspiring take away that you remember that kept you focused on your goals! Write it down so you can reflect back to it from time to time!

What is glowing within you right now on this 29th day?

_____
_____
_____

Today's thoughts/reflections.

_____
_____
_____

Today's goals completed:

_____
_____
_____

Today's accomplishments/gratitude:

_____
_____
_____

DATE: _____

DAY 30

Congratulations on a job well done! Celebrate all your self-care successes, self-loved ways, accomplishments, and goals reached in becoming a beautiful New You!

THESE 30 DAYS WERE...

challenging because:

_____
_____
_____
_____

beneficial because:

_____
_____
_____
_____

rewarding because:

_____
_____
_____
_____

rejuvenating because:

_____
_____
_____
_____

The New Version of YOU

Learn from Yesterday, live for today, hope for
tomorrow...

ALBERT EINSTEIN

Congratulations! You have started a self-care journey by completing your 30-day challenge. You persisted because you knew that all your hard work would bring the reward of a healthier you!

During the last 30 days, you have changed your life by investing time in yourself. During your self-care journey, you may have learned that making a meaningful change in your life can be anxiety provoking. We know that change doesn't happen in an instant. If change is going to last and become a new habit, you will need to continue to practice it daily. Taking on too many changes at once can be overwhelming and not successful. Speaking from experience it's best to take small steps as they are more manageable and give the best outcomes. You may already have discovered this through the challenge.

This is not the end of your self-care journey, it's just the beginning. Self-care is a life style choice that must become part of your daily routine in order for it to become long term and successful! Celebrate all your self-care goals, set-backs, obstacles and disappointments. You worked hard to balance your successes and failures for health recovery. Don't forget that the trying moments are what got you here. Look at yourself in the mirror and meet, "The New Version of You".

A true self-care journey takes a commitment to persevere no matter what the challenges! Most importantly, your mind, body and spirit all need to be continually nourished and replenished! Never stop thinking about you! If you don't take care of yourself, how can you accomplish any of your life goals?

A dōTERRA Essential Oil Specialist

I would like to share the main reason I've become a dōTERRA Essential oil specialist. My personal self-care journey was to find a natural solution for my thyroid condition. What I learned was that dōTERRA is the number one global leader in essential oils and aromatherapy. When you use a bottle of dōTERRA essential oil you are using an oil that is pure, with no contaminants, filers or adulterations. The essential oils industry did not have standards to ensure purity, so dōTERRA was the first to create the purity standards in the world today.

Becoming a dōTERRA independent Wellness advocate for 8 years now has given me a platform to illustrate and educate how wellness is a combination of lifestyle and healthcare. When lifestyle is the focus, health is naturally achieved and maintained. When the opportunity came to join the dōTERRA essential oil family it was a privilege to be part of their dynamic essential oil world. dōTERRA family has one of the most professional and generous teams you'd want as your legacy. On a daily basis my health benefits using these 100% pure and powerful dōTERRA essential oils have improved my physical, emotional, intellectual and spiritual well-being. dōTERRA means, "Gift of the Earth". For me it means healing, hope and wellness.

Essential oils are natural aromatic compounds that are distilled from plants including seeds, bark, leaves, stems, roots, flowers, fruit and trees. Present in a pure, concentrated form these compounds have medicinal properties that have been utilized for centuries in the field of plant-based therapy. dōTERRA essential oils are unequivocally pure, concentrated, and strongly supported by scientific evidence.

Three ways to use dōTERRA essential oils:

* INTERNAL: which only certified pure grade essential oils are taken internally. Take directly by mouth either with veggie capsule or water. For internal use check for the supplement facts on the label.

* AROMATIC: use an essential oil diffuser or inhale directly. This way it cleanses the air, opens airways and affects the moods.

* TOPICAL: can use by applying to the bottom of the feet which can enter circulatory system within 30 seconds. Can also apply to other localized areas. Dilute with a carrier oil such as fractioned coconut oil which helps absorbed the oils more or if you have sensitive skin.

How can these essential oils support the body? Essential oils decrease stress, support a healthy immune system and joint function. Also, can promote a healthy metabolism, relaxation, and emotional health; detox the body systems, improve skin irritations, maintain healthy circulation and so much more!

Consider the major benefits of essential oils in supporting your self-care journey with the daily use of these natural aromatic oils. When using essential oils consistently, they can enhance and support your daily total well-being.

dōTERRA essential oils do not prevent, treat or cure disease. Your healthy lifestyle choices help prevent disease. Your body cures disease! When you give your body what it needs it heals itself.

The Role of a Health-Wellness Coach

Wellness coaches are credentialed health, fitness, and mental health professionals. Who may coach clients on areas of nutrition, fitness, weight loss, mental and emotional fitness (stress, anxiety or sleep etc.) or other health issues that may impact wellness using evidence base strategies?

Coaching is a close relationship and partnership that provides structure, accountability, expertise and inspiration to enable an individual to learn, grow and develop beyond what he or she can do alone. The coach creates an environment through conversation and a way of being mindfully present that facilitates the process by which the individual can set goals and be successful.

Today, coaches are valuable in other different areas to assist individuals in navigating their way through some life transition such as: career change, retirement, time management, improving health conditions or finding a new sense of work-life passion and purpose. Corporations hire coaches to improve the performance of their executives or managers. Key strategies in the coach-client partnership include having a focus on building self-efficacy and empowerment by providing thoughtful reflections. Asking non-judgmental questions and being that co-creative partner in the client's journey enables one to reach their wellness vision and goals.

Becoming a health-wellness coach has been a natural path born from my many years of nursing experiences. Not only has it further developed my own expertise but has helped several individuals to keep a focus on aligning personal health goals and values to improve their well-being.

We all share the need to partner with a coach to guide and collaborate along the healing journey if our hope is to live a well-balanced lifestyle. One of my colleague's once shared with me, "Even the best coaches need coaching in order to be our best selves." How does this resonate with you? Has there ever been a time in your life or a family member's life that needed a coach to help them with a health issue?

As a health-wellness coach I utilize **3 core skills** when coaching clients. These provide a unique coaching partnership to find solutions and overcome obstacles which gives the client total focus on what they want to change, achieve and reach their goals.

THREE CORE RELATIONSHIP SKILLS ARE THE TOOLS FOR BEING THE BEST COACH!

#1. MINDFUL LISTENING. This is the most important of all my coaching skills. Listening brings full, non-judgmental awareness of what someone is saying in the present moment. Always listen to the words and the truth beyond the words. Listen to facts, feelings and needs behind the facts.

#2. OPEN ENDED INQUIRY. Avoid asking too many questions for the client may feel interrogated. Best to start with the what and how questions. Use the "why" questions when connecting with the client's deepest motivators. I believe these questions elicit what is on the client's mind and not what's on the coach's mind.

#3. PERCEPTIVE REFLECTIONS. This is another form of listening. The simplest reflection is to restate what a client says in their own words. This allows the client to see themselves more clearly and moves them forward to engage in search of a higher well-being and be their "best-self".

My health-wellness coach approach is to stimulate individual behavior change. It focuses on helping them grow into becoming experts of their own well-being; encouraging personal responsibility, self-discovery, confidence, motivation and self-efficacy. These build on what's working instead of what's not. Partner with a wellness coach to begin your healthy journey today!

Personal Notes

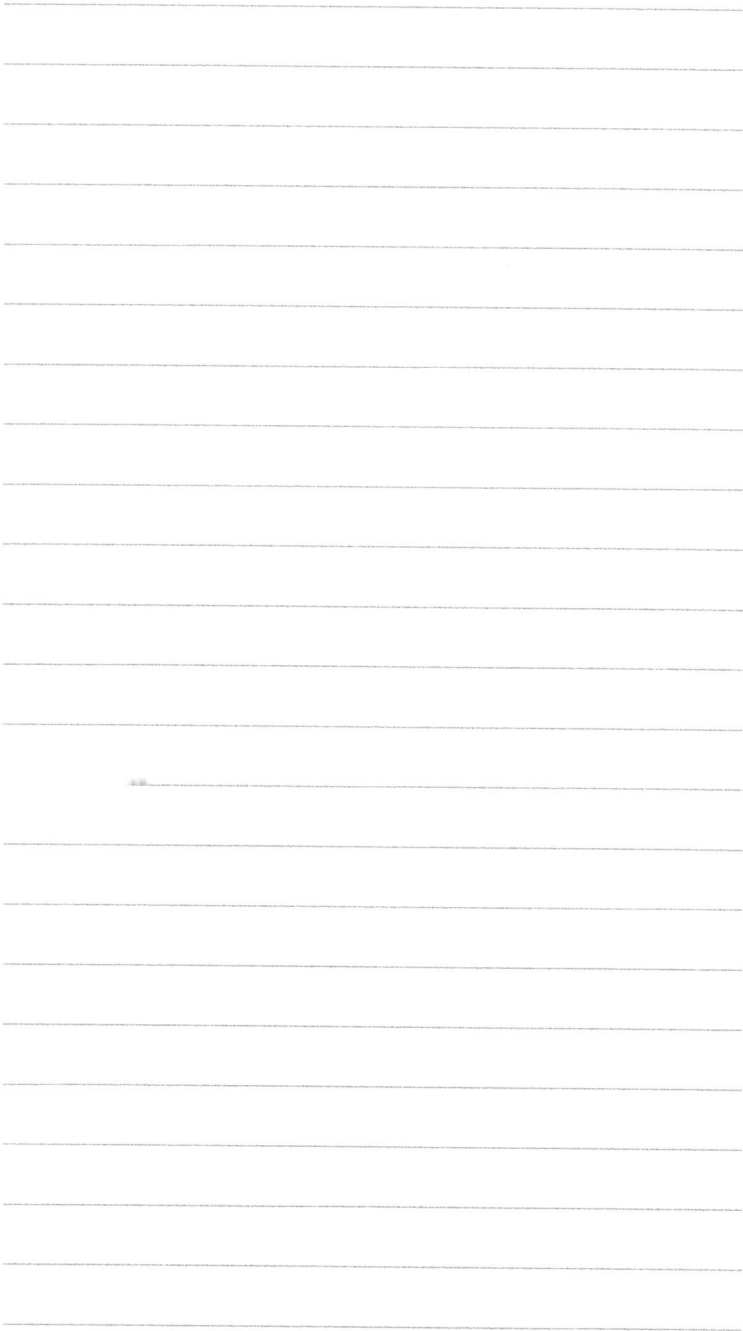

Acknowledgments

Special thanks to my daughters, Kristie, Marsha, Tricia; grandchildren Zachary, Davis and Marisa. If it weren't for all of you this book would not exist. All your love, enthusiasm and support this past year was heartwarming. You certainly kept me inspired to create this self-care journal to share with the world.

My family and friends from the east to the west coast who have journeyed with me from start to finish in writing this book. You have given constant encouragement, inspiration and advice throughout this past year. For my heart is so grateful to each one of you.

So grateful, for my dōTERRA Essential Oil team who have given me inspiration, training, guidance and knowledge in using essential oils for past 8 years that has enhanced my wellness lifestyle.

Cousin Beatrice, so grateful and blessed to have had you help editing and your timely guidance and suggestions to create the right book format. We agreed that this 30-day challenge will change many individuals' lives.

Jean Shorey, so appreciative and grateful for all your help, time and support this past year guiding me to complete this self-care journal book. You are an amazing, talented and gifted artist

Alicia Girard, special thanks for your expertise in graphic design and drafting the first step in my book venture with me.

So grateful, Steven Couture for all your IT work but especially your efficiency and expertise with high-quality computer programming.

About the Author

Maine native born and raised in Waterville, Maine into a family of five children. I have raised my own family of 3 daughters and 3 grandchildren here in this picture-perfect state. The coast of Maine has always been a lifeline for me because of the tranquility and peace it brings for my own self-care journey.

My life's work as a registered nurse and certified health-wellness coach have taken me along the path of holistic healing with the combined use of essential oils and integrative medicine. We all need knowledge to be able to heal our own bodies, whether due to a physical or emotional imbalance or a combination of these two crucial aspects of the whole person!

I have worked with a diverse population of individuals living with acute and chronic illnesses. My coaching approach is to empower each person to live a healthy lifestyle by building on a foundation of proper nutrition, exercise, rest and reversing toxic exposure. The most important part of the healing journey is our first line of defense in developing self-care rituals and habits in order to maintain a healthy lifestyle.

Working as a nurse and health coach helping individuals meet their medical needs or creating their own self-care journey can be challenging at times. It is also very rewarding! Making a difference in the lives of my clients is my main purpose as a health care provider. Helping others create a lifestyle balance of physical, emotional, intellectual and spiritual lives has been my life's passion and reward!

Becoming a dōTERRA Independent Wellness advocate nearly 8 years ago has given me a platform to illustrate and educate how wellness is a combination of lifestyle and healthcare. When lifestyle is the focus, health is naturally achieved and maintained. Memories of my grandmother using the bark of trees and plants from her gardens to make liniments as holistic methods to manage her health care. When the opportunity came to join the dōTERRA essential oil family it was a privilege to be part of their dynamic world. dōTERRA family has one of the most unified, professional and generous teams that you want as your legacy. My health benefits on a daily basis using these 100% pure and powerful dōTERRA essential oils have improved my physical, emotional and spiritual well-being. dōTERRA means, "Gift of the Earth". For me it means healing, hope and wellness.

References

ADVANCED OIL MAGIC by Oil Magic
(Cheyenne, WY: 2019 first printing updated)
Advanced Oil Magic brings the balance of essential magic and science. The magic is in the protocols. The science backs it up.

EAT TO LIVE by Dr. Joel Fuhrman, MD
(New York: Little Brown and Company, 2011)
This new revised edition includes inspiring success stories who lost large amount of weight and recovered from life threatening illnesses.

GREEN FOR LIFE by Victoria Boutenko
(Canada: 2005)
Victoria gives us a unique, yet simple and delicious strategy for boosting our nutritional levels.

GREEN SMOOTHIES FOR DUMMIES by Jennifer Thompson
(Hoboken, NJ: John Wiley & Sons, Inc. 2014)
Sip your way to ultimate nutrition and feel better than ever with green smoothies

HERBS FOR HEALTH AND HEALING by Kathi Keville with Peter Korn
(US: Friedman Group, 1996)
Even though this book was written 20 plus years ago it has safe and simple formulas for dozens of health problems.

LIFE MAKEOVERS by Cheryl Richardson
(New York: Broadway books, 2000)

The "Life Makeover" ...How often do you daydream about living a better life-a life that reflects more of you, your values and deepest desires?

MODERN ESSENTIALS EIGHT EDITION by Aroma Tools
(UT: 2016AromaTools)

This unique guide can help you discover how essential oils can benefit your health and well-being naturally!

ORGANIZE YOUR MIND ORGANIZE YOUR LIFE by Paul Hammerness, MD & Margaret Moore with John Hanc
(Canada: Harlequinnbooks, 2012)

This groundbreaking guide is complete with stories of people who have learned to stop feeling powerless against multiplying distractions and start organizing their minds.

THE GOOD GUT by Justin Sonnenburg and Erica Sonnenburg, PhDs
(New York: Penguin books, 2016)

Justin and Erica Sonnenburg are pioneers in one of the most exciting fields of human health and wellness today.

THE TAPPING SOLUTION by Nick Ortner
(US: Hay House, Inc. 1st edition, April 2013)

Tapping, also known as EFT, is a powerful tool for improving your life on multiple levels; mental, emotional and physical.

THE COMPLETE ILLUSTRATED GUIDE TO REFLEXOLOGY
(London: Barnes & Noble Books, 1996)

The history of reflexology and the importance of its holistic approach. It is an indispensable tool for self-treatment and basic techniques.

THE HEALING POWER OF ESSENTIAL OILS by Eric Zielinski, D.C.
(NY: Penguin Random House LLC, 2018)

Soothe inflammation, boost mood, prevent autoimmunity and feel great in every way.

YOGA THREE IN ONE
(Australia: 2006, Hinkle books)

Three complete home workout programs.

YOU CAN HEAL YOUR LIFE by Louise L. Hay
(CA: Hay House Inc, 2000)

Louise key message is: "If you are ready to do the mental work, almost anything can be healed."

Resources

1. www.healthylifestylecoaching.org

2. www.everydayhealth.com

3. www.livestrong.com

4. www.nourishedkitchen.com

5. www.womenhealthnetwork.com

6. www.autoimmunestrong.com

7. www.healthyhappinessforever.com

8. www.mindbodygreen.com

9. www.hellochopra.com

10. www.healthversed.com

11. www.doterra.com

12. www.mindfulness.com

13. www.positivepsychology.com

14. www.healthline.com

15. www.indeedcareerguide.com

16. www.healthybliss.net

17. www.xpcconsulting.com

www.ingramcontent.com/pod-product-compliance
Lightning Source LLC
Chambersburg PA
CBHW070028030426
42335CB00017B/2343